spot

OCEAN ANIMALS

D0815258

SEA TURTLES

by Mari Schuh

AMICUS | AMICUS INK

flipper

shell

Look for these words and pictures as you read.

beak

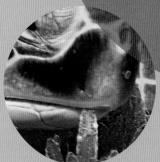

eggs

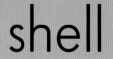

A sea turtle dives.
See it go!

Sea turtles are reptiles.
They have scales.
They have lungs.

Look at the flipper.
A sea turtle has four.
They help it swim.

flipper

Look at the hard shell.
It is made of bone.
It keeps sea turtles
safe from enemies.

shell

Look at its beak.

It grabs crabs to eat.

It tears apart seagrass to eat.

beak

eggs

Look at the eggs.
A female lays eggs in a nest.
She covers them with sand.

After eight weeks, the eggs hatch.
The young grow.
Soon they will swim and dive!

Look at the flipper.
A sea turtle has four.
They help it swim.

flipper

flipper

Look at the hard shell.
It is made of bone.
It keeps sea turtles
safe from enemies.

shell

shell

Did you find?

beak

eggs

Look at its beak.
It grabs crabs to eat.
It tears apart seagrass to eat.

beak

Look at the eggs.
A female lays eggs in a nest.
She covers them with sand.

eggs

Spot is published by Amicus and Amicus Ink
P.O. Box 1329, Mankato, MN 56002
www.amicuspublishing.us

Copyright © 2019 Amicus.
International copyright reserved in all countries.
No part of this book may be reproduced in any form
without written permission from the publisher.

Library of Congress Cataloging-in-Publication Data
Names: Schuh, Mari C., 1975- author.
Title: Sea turtles / by Mari Schuh.
Description: Mankato, Minnesota : Amicus, [2019] | Series:
  Spot. Ocean animals | Audience: K to grade 3.
Identifiers: LCCN 2017020473 (print) | LCCN 2017043884
  (ebook) | ISBN 9781681514642 (eBook) |
  ISBN 9781681513829 (library binding) |
  ISBN 9781681523026 (pbk.)
Subjects: LCSH: Sea turtles--Juvenile literature. | Marine
  animals--Juvenile literature.
Classification: LCC QL666.C536 (ebook) | LCC QL666
  C536 S356 2019 (print) | DDC 597.92/8--dc23
LC record available at https://lccn.loc.gov/2017020473

Printed in China

HC 10 9 8 7 6 5 4 3 2 1
PB 10 9 8 7 6 5 4 3 2 1

Rebecca Glaser, editor
Deb Miner, series designer
Ciara Beitlich, book designer
Holly Young, photo researcher

Photos by AgeFotostock/Gerard Lacz,
12–13; iStock/babelfilm, 1, richcarey,
10–11, italiansight, 14–15; Shutterstock/
Rich Carey, cover, 6–7, Dmitry Laudin, 3,
Andrey Armyagov, 4–5, Neophuket, 8–9

SEA TURTLES